CONTINENTS

AFRICA

by Alicia Klepeis

Content Consultant
Anne Jebet Waliaula, PhD
Outreach Coordinator, African Studies Program
Lecturer, African Languages and Literature

CORE
LIBRARY

Published by ABDO Publishing Company, PO Box 398166, Minneapolis, MN 55439. Copyright © 2014 by Abdo Consulting Group, Inc. International copyrights reserved in all countries. No part of this book may be reproduced in any form without written permission from the publisher. The Core Library™ is a trademark and logo of ABDO Publishing Company.

Printed in the United States of America,
North Mankato, Minnesota
042013
012014

♻ THIS BOOK CONTAINS AT LEAST 10% RECYCLED MATERIALS.

Editor: Blythe Hurley
Series Designer: Becky Daum

Library of Congress Control Number: 2013931967

Cataloging-in-Publication Data
Klepeis, Alicia.
 Africa / Alicia Klepeis.
   p. cm. -- (Continents)
ISBN 978-1-61783-928-3 (lib. bdg.)
ISBN 978-1-61783-993-1 (pbk.)
1. Africa--Juvenile literature.   I. Title.
916--dc23
                                    2013931967

CONTENTS

Quick Facts about Africa 4

CHAPTER ONE
Introduction to Africa 6

CHAPTER TWO
Landforms, Bodies of Water,
and Climate 12

CHAPTER THREE
Plants and Animals 18

CHAPTER FOUR
African History 24

CHAPTER FIVE
The People of Africa 30

CHAPTER SIX
Africa Today 36

Places to See 42
Stop and Think 44
Glossary. 46
Learn More. 47
Index 48
About the Author 48

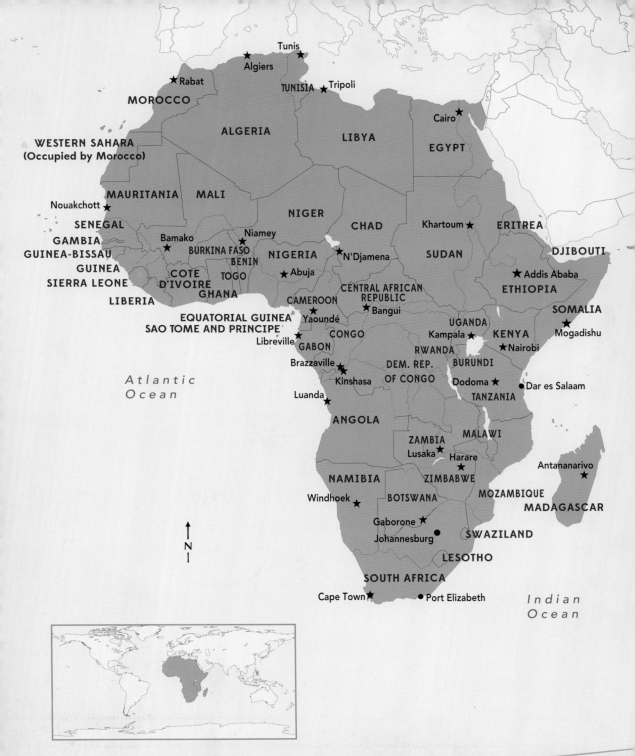

QUICK FACTS ABOUT AFRICA

- **Highest point:** Mount Kilimanjaro, Tanzania, 19,340 feet (5,895 m)
- **Area:** 11,608,000 square miles (30,064,582 sq km)
- **Distance north to south:** 4,800 miles (7,725 km)
- **Distance east to west:** 4,500 miles (7,242 km)
- **Key industries:** agriculture, chemicals, mining, cement
- **Population:** 1,072,254,100
- **Five biggest cities:** Lagos, Nigeria; Cairo, Egypt; Kinshasa, Democratic Republic of the Congo; Alexandria, Egypt; Abidjan, Cote D'Ivoire
- **Three most common languages:** Arabic, English, Swahili
- **Number of countries:** 54

CHAPTER ONE

INTRODUCTION TO AFRICA

When people think about Africa, lions and elephants roaming vast grasslands come to mind. But Africa is so much more than wildlife. It is full of richness from coast to coast. Africa has a great deal of variety. Tropical rainforests, grasslands called savannas, and deserts are just a few of Africa's environments. Many people follow ancient ways of life, while others live in modern

Tanzania's Ngorongoro Crater is known for its large population of wildlife.

cities. There is no one environment or culture in Africa.

Tourists to this continent can sail the world's longest river, the Nile. They can travel across the Sahara, the world's largest non-polar desert. They can climb Africa's tallest mountain, Mount Kilimanjaro, which is often capped with snow.

Water surrounds much of Africa. The Atlantic Ocean, Indian Ocean, Red Sea, and Mediterranean Sea border its coasts.

Africa's Size

After Asia, Africa is the second-largest continent in size and population.

The Sahara: A Changing Landscape

Fifteen thousand years ago, the Sahara Desert was even drier than it is today. But nine thousand years ago, the Sahara was quite different. It had savannas, rivers, lakes, and woodlands. People planted crops and herded livestock there. By 2500 BCE the rains in North Africa had decreased, and the Sahara Desert as we know it began to form. Today the Sahara Desert has golden sand dunes that extend as far as the eye can see.

The city of Cairo, which is the capital of Egypt, was founded more than 1,000 years ago.

The continental United States could fit inside Africa's Sahara Desert. The Sahara is just part of Africa's huge landmass. More than 1 billion people live in Africa.

Ancient Africa

Africa is the oldest of the seven continents. South Africa contains rocks that are billions of years old.

Some people still use camels to travel in Africa's many deserts.

People often call Africa the cradle of human life. Scientists have found that our species, *Homo sapiens*, first appeared in Africa about 200,000 years ago. Humans have built tools and lived off the land in Africa for many thousands of years.

Today nomads roaming the desert and city dwellers driving to work all call Africa home. Africans have created art and music that people enjoy around the world. People from many cultures live on this amazing continent.

CHAPTER TWO

LANDFORMS, BODIES OF WATER, AND CLIMATE

Africa covers 11,608,000 square miles (30,064,582 sq km) of land. It takes up about one-fifth of Earth's surface. About half of the continent is above the equator, while the other half is below it.

Africa's center is a green band of tropical rainforests and grasslands. The south receives much less rain. The north is mostly desert.

Tanzania is home to lush rainforests bursting with plant and animal life.

African Environments

Africa has many deserts. The Sahara is the world's largest non-polar desert. It stretches across northern Africa, covering about 25 percent of the continent. The Sahara's ergs, or sand dunes, are miles long. They can reach heights of more than 1,000 feet (305 m) tall!

The Sahel is a plains region. It lies between the Sahara and the savannas to the south. The Niger River flows through the Sahel.

Savannas cover nearly half of Africa. Grasslands make up much of central Africa's landscape. The Serengeti Plain is a famous African savanna region. It is home to huge animal populations.

Life in an Oasis

An oasis is a fertile place where water is found in a desert. The water in an oasis may come from a spring, well, or irrigation system. About 75 percent of the population in the Sahara Desert lives in oases. The Siwa Oasis lies in the western desert of Egypt. Siwa's water sources allow palm groves, olive orchards, and date plantations to thrive. Siwa's 30,000 residents have found ways to live in the middle of the harsh desert.

Mount Kilimanjaro, Africa's tallest mountain, is a dormant volcano.

Mount Kilimanjaro lies on the border between Kenya and Tanzania. Other mountainous areas in Africa include the Atlas Mountains in northwestern Africa and the Ethiopian Highlands in eastern Africa. The climate in these areas is cooler than in other parts of Africa.

The Great Rift Valley is an area of tectonic activity. This means sections of the Earth's crust, called plates, are moving apart deep underground. The Great Rift Valley has volcanoes, hot springs, geysers, and

These Malian women are selling fish caught in the Niger River.

earthquakes. Africa's Great Lakes are located in and around this valley too. They include Lake Tanganyika and Lake Victoria, two of the world's largest lakes.

The Climates of Africa

Africa's climates range from very wet to very dry. Near the equator, there is heavy rainfall year round. There are also cooler and warmer seasons. The savannas have distinct wet and dry seasons. The northern and southern coasts have milder, subtropical climates. Africa's desert areas are extremely dry. They receive less than ten inches (25 cm) of rain per year.

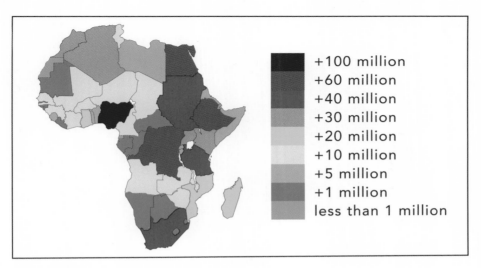

	+100 million
	+60 million
	+40 million
	+30 million
	+20 million
	+10 million
	+5 million
	+1 million
	less than 1 million

Population in Africa

This map shows where people live in Africa. How does the information presented compare to what you have learned in Chapter Two? Which areas are the most and least crowded? Why do you think this is the case?

Where People Live

Access to water and fertile soil affects where people choose to live in Africa. Places with fertile soil have the largest populations. For example, more than 90 percent of Egypt's population lives within a few miles of the life-giving Nile River. Many people also live along Africa's coasts. There they have access to trading centers and transportation. Others live near lakes and rivers, which contain fish to eat and water to drink.

CHAPTER THREE

PLANTS AND ANIMALS

From its savannas to its tropical rainforests, Africa is home to a huge variety of plants and animals.

Africa's Plant Life

Tropical rainforests once covered most of central Africa. People have destroyed much of this native rainforest with logging, farming, and development. Today most of Africa's rainforest is centered on the

Baobab trees on the island nation of Madagascar

Baobab Trees

The baobab tree is often called "the upside-down tree." This is because its branches look like roots sticking up in the air. Baobab trees grow in dry areas of Africa and Australia. Their gigantic trunks store huge amounts of water. This allows baobab trees to survive in times of drought. Baobab trees can live for more than 1,500 years. Baobabs produce large, pod-like fruit that is sometimes called monkey bread. This fruit is rich in vitamin C. People use baobab leaves for medicine. They make rope, cloth, and nets by shredding the tree's bark.

Congo River basin. There are an estimated 8,000 plant species in Africa's rainforests.

African savannas feature tall grasses and thorny bushes. Acacia, baobab, and manketti trees thrive in this environment.

Few types of plants grow in Africa's deserts. Desert plants have deep root systems that help them survive the extreme conditions. Plants known as succulents store water in their leaves.

Okapis are shy creatures of Africa's central rainforests.

Animals of Africa

Gorillas, parrots, monkeys, and okapis are just some of the animals that call Africa's tropical rainforests home. Many kinds of snakes, frogs, birds, and butterflies also live here.

Africa's grasslands are home to huge animal populations. Many of Africa's largest animals live here. These include rhinoceroses and giraffes. On the Serengeti Plain, massive herds of wildebeests, zebras,

Madagascar

Madagascar is an island off the eastern coast of Africa. It broke away from the rest of the continent between 100 and 200 million years ago. Madagascar's plants and animals have developed on their own since then. They are very different from those on the mainland. Many species of lemurs live on this island. Nearly half of the world's chameleon species live on Madagascar. Chameleons are lizards with skin that changes color in response to light, temperature, and the animals' moods.

and gazelles migrate in search of food and water. The Serengeti Plain lies in Tanzania to the west of the Great Rift Valley.

Africa's deserts might seem too harsh for animal life. However, many desert creatures have adapted to extremely dry conditions. For example, scorpions hunt at night. They burrow beneath the desert sand to stay cool during the day. Dromedary camels can change their body temperature. This helps them conserve water by preventing the camels from sweating in the heat of the day.

Lemurs, like this mother and her young, live only in Madagascar.

FURTHER EVIDENCE

There is quite a bit of information about African animals in Chapter Three. What was one of the chapter's main points? What are some pieces of evidence in the chapter that support this main point? Go to the article on African rainforest animals at the Web site below. Does the information on this Web site support the main point in this chapter? Write a few sentences using new information from the Web site as evidence to support the main point in this chapter.

African Rainforest Animals

www.mycorelibrary.com/africa

CHAPTER FOUR

AFRICAN HISTORY

K nown as the cradle of human life, Africa has a long history. Scientists called archaeologists have learned how humans developed from our apelike ancestors who lived in Africa 7 million years ago.

Ancient African Civilizations

Africa is the oldest inhabited continent on Earth. It has been home to many civilizations. Ancient Egyptians

The Temple of Osiris is one of many ancient Egyptian structures that still stands today.

The Great Sphinx of Giza, Egypt, with the Pyramid of Khufu in the background, is believed to be more than 4,000 years old.

had a highly developed culture. They created detailed works of art, built temples and pyramids, and used a writing system called hieroglyphics.

From the 400s to the 1500s CE, several West African empires thrived. These empires had advanced trade networks, armies, and taxation systems.

European Involvement in Africa

During the 1400s, Europeans started exploring Africa. At first they explored only along Africa's coasts. By the 1700s, however, Europeans began exploring Africa's interior.

Several European countries sent ships to Africa. These nations built forts and settlements. Europeans traded with Africans for gold, ivory, and spices. They also began trading for slaves to work in the New World. Between the 1400s and 1800s, Europeans brought more than 15 million Africans to the Americas to be sold as slaves.

During the late 1800s, France, Great Britain, Germany, and

Great Zimbabwe

Great Zimbabwe was the site of a powerful ancient city in sub-Saharan Africa, which is the part of Africa south of the Sahara Desert. Built between 1100 and 1450 CE, Great Zimbabwe was an important trading center. The city's people traded porcelain, cloth, and glass for gold and ivory. At its height, Great Zimbabwe was home to between 12,000 and 20,000 people.

Captured Africans were often forced to march for long distances before being sold as slaves.

other European countries claimed most of Africa as colonies of their own. They drew boundaries that did not consider the interests or traditions of the African people. European rulers took control of Africa's natural resources. During the late 1900s, most African nations achieved independence.

Many African nations have faced great challenges since the colonial period. For example, after South Africa won its independence from Great Britain in 1961, a policy called apartheid discriminated against the country's nonwhite citizens. Today Africa's independent nations are working to improve life for all of their citizens.

In 1994 Nelson Mandela became the first democratically elected president in South African history. He was also the first black president after more than three centuries of white rule. The excerpt below is from his inaugural speech:

> *The time for the healing of the wounds has come.*
>
> *The moment to bridge the chasms that divide us has come.*
>
> *The time to build is upon us. . . .*
>
> *We have, at last, achieved our political emancipation. . . . We have triumphed in the effort to implant hope in the breasts of the millions of our people. We enter into a covenant that we shall build the society in which all South Africans, both black and white, will be able to walk tall, without any fear in their hearts, assured of their inalienable right to human dignity—a rainbow nation at peace with itself and the world.*

Source: Nelson Mandela. "Inaugural Speech, Pretoria [Mandela]- 5/10/94." University of Pennsylvania - African Studies Center. University of Pennsylvania, May 10, 1994. Web. Accessed February 18, 2013.

What's the Big Idea?

Take a close look at this speech. What is Mandela's main point about South Africa's past and its future? Pick out two details he uses to make this point. What can you tell about the population of South Africa based on this speech?

CHAPTER FIVE

THE PEOPLE OF AFRICA

Africa is home to many cultural and ethnic groups. Each has their own customs and beliefs. Some people follow the traditions of their ancestors. Others live in modern cities.

African Music and Dance

Music is part of everyday life in many African cultures. Drums are especially important in African music.

A member of the Maasai ethnic group in Kenya wears traditional decorations and clothing.

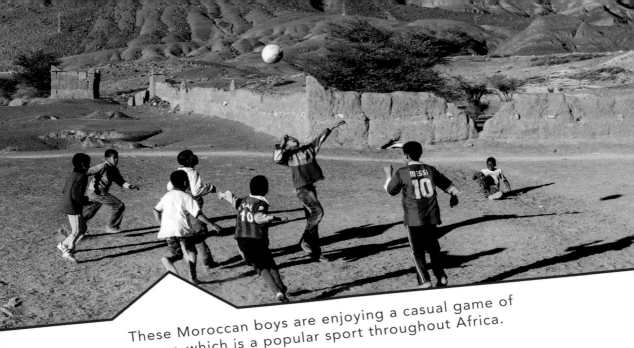

These Moroccan boys are enjoying a casual game of soccer, which is a popular sport throughout Africa.

Dance is also an important part of many African cultures. People often celebrate marriages, births, and even funerals with dancing.

Sports in Africa

Soccer is by far the most popular sport in Africa. Most people there call it football. In 2010 South Africa became the first African nation to host the International Federation of Association Football (FIFA) World Cup. Other common sports include cricket, basketball, wrestling, volleyball, rugby, and track and field.

Life in Africa's Cities

Africa's cities are growing rapidly and becoming more modern. But many urban Africans still live in slums. These are extremely poor areas where people build their homes using any materials they can find.

Rural African Life

Most Africans live in the countryside. Many are farmers who grow food crops, including corn, yams, or millet. They may raise livestock, such as sheep or cows. Families may live in compounds made up of several houses with a meeting place or courtyard in the center.

Maasai Style

Among the Maasai people of Kenya and Tanzania, men wear their hair in long braids, which they dye with red clay. Women and children shave their heads. The Maasai are known for their colorful beadwork. These beads share information about the person wearing them. For example, you can tell if a Maasai woman is married, if she has children, and how wealthy she is by the number of beaded necklaces she wears.

Nomads of Africa

In the drier parts of Africa, people often live a nomadic lifestyle. This means they move from place to place rather than living in a permanent home. The Tuareg people live in the Sahara Desert. They live in tents that can be set up and taken down easily so they can move with their goats, camels, and sheep. The San people live in the Kalahari Desert. They hunt game and gather fruits and other food.

Communication and Religion

More than 1,000 languages are spoken across Africa. Arabic is widely spoken in northern Africa. Swahili is common in eastern and central Africa. Millions of African people speak more than one language.

Religious beliefs vary across Africa. Most people in northern Africa are Muslim. Other parts of Africa have more Christians. Many African people still practice traditional religions. Each of Africa's religions has its own celebrations, rituals, and views about the world.

In 2004 environmentalist Wangari Maathai won the Nobel Peace Prize. In her acceptance speech, she spoke about changes to Kenya's natural areas that have taken place during her lifetime:

> *I reflect on my childhood experience when I would visit a stream next to our home to fetch water for my mother. I would drink water straight from the stream. . . . I tried in vain to pick up the strands of frogs' eggs. . . . Later, I saw thousands of tadpoles. . . . This is the world I inherited from my parents.*
>
> *Today, over 50 years later, the stream has dried up, women walk long distances for water, which is not always clean, and children will never know what they have lost. The challenge is to restore the home of the tadpoles and give back to our children a world of beauty and wonder.*

Source: Wangari Maathai. "The Nobel Peace Prize 2004/Wangari Maathai." Nobelprize.org: The Official Website of the Nobel Prize. Nobel Media, December 10, 2004. Web. Accessed February 18, 2013.

What's the Big Idea?

In her speech, Wangari Maathai used evidence to support a point. Write a paragraph describing the point she is making. Then write down two or three pieces of evidence she uses to support her point.

CHAPTER SIX

AFRICA TODAY

African people do all kinds of work, from farming to teaching to scientific research. There are two main types of farming in Africa. Subsistence farmers grow food only for their own family's needs. Millions of people in Africa are subsistence farmers. However, people in Africa also grow cash crops. This means they sell their crops at market or to other buyers. In Africa's tropical areas,

The bustling market of Aswan in southern Egypt is a popular destination for locals and tourists.

Many tourists visit Africa every year to see its stunning landscapes and wildlife.

rubber and palm oil are important cash crops. So is cacao, the seed used to make chocolate. In drier parts of Africa, farmers grow peanuts and cotton. In the highland areas, they grow coffee.

Tourism

For many African nations, tourism is an important source of jobs and income. Visitors from around

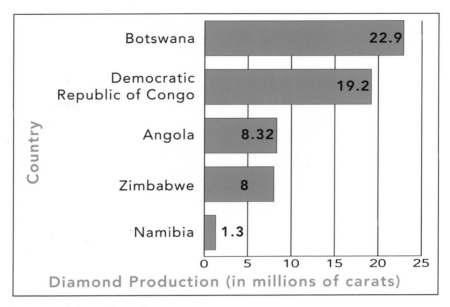

Diamond Production

This graph shows diamond production for the top six diamond-producing countries in Africa in millions of carats. A carat is a unit of weight for precious stones, metals, and similar materials. How does the information in this graph compare to the information about natural resources in Chapter Six? What problems might these African countries face if the demand for diamonds fell?

the globe come to see Africa's landscapes, wildlife, historical sites, and indigenous cultures.

Africa's Natural Resources

Africa is a source of some of the world's most precious metals and minerals. This includes gold, copper, and diamonds. Other natural resources include oil, natural

Schoolboys orphaned by HIV/AIDS in Swaziland hope to achieve a brighter future through education.

gas, timber, and coal. Many African countries struggle to manage these resources.

African Governments

The governments of Africa vary widely. In some countries, such as Senegal, people vote for the people they want to run their country. Other African nations, including Zimbabwe, are run by dictators. This means a single person has complete control over the country. Dictators often limit their citizens' rights and freedoms.

Africa's Future

Africa faces many challenges. Overcoming poverty is one of its main issues. And diseases such as AIDS and malaria continue to threaten the health of Africa's people. Some of Africa's fertile lands are becoming deserts due to overgrazing, lack of rainfall, and the clearing of vegetation for farming. Demand for lumber and firewood is leading to the destruction of Africa's forests.

Still, people are making progress across Africa. For example, in sub-Saharan Africa, the number of students in high school more than doubled between 1999 and 2010. Africans are working hard to build a better future for their continent.

Malaria

Malaria is a disease spread through the bite of infected mosquitoes. Sub-Saharan Africa has more cases of malaria than any other part of the world. But Malaria can be prevented and cured. Sleeping under mosquito nets treated with insecticide is one way to prevent the spread of malaria. Another way is to spray insecticides in houses. There are also anti-malaria medicines.

San tribespeople

Kruger National Park, South Africa

Kruger National Park is home to black and white rhinos, cheetahs, elephants, and warthogs. Visitors can also see ancient rock paintings made by the San people.

Seychelles

This small nation is paradise for tourists. Scuba divers and snorkelers can explore more than 115 coral and granite islands.

Snorkeling in La Digue, Seychelles

Djenné, Mali

This ancient city was a trading center for caravan routes crossing the Sahara Desert.

A mud mosque in Djenné, Mali

The Lagos River

Victoria Falls

Spices for sale at the Marrakech market

Lagos, Nigeria

Africa's largest city is full of people, traffic, and businesses. The city struggles with meeting the housing, sanitation, and transportation needs of its residents.

Victoria Falls

Located on the border between Zambia and Zimbabwe, Victoria Falls is one of the largest waterfalls on Earth.

Marrakech, Morocco

Marrakech's bustling market square is called Djemaa el Fna. Here you will see snake charmers, musicians, scribes, and more.

Why Do I Care?

Ancient Egyptians may have lived long ago, but your life may not be as different from an ancient Egyptian's as you think. Do you ever create artwork to share messages with your friends and family? Have you ever attended a church, synagogue, or temple to gather with others from your community? What was it like? Write down two or three ways that the ancient Egyptians and their way of life connect to your life.

Take a Stand

This book discusses how European countries claimed Africa's natural resources during colonial rule. Do you think colonial rulers should have been allowed to sell Africa's resources? Should they have given the local people control over them? Write a short essay explaining your opinion. Be sure to give reasons for your opinion and facts and details to support those reasons.

You Are There

This book discusses Africa's nomadic people. Imagine you are a Tuareg boy or a girl in the Sahara. You must move regularly to keep your animals fed and watered. Do you like always being on the move? What are the challenges and benefits of a nomadic lifestyle?

Say What?

Studying another continent can mean learning many new words. Find five words in this book that you have never heard before. Use a dictionary to find out what they mean. Then write the meanings in your own words, and use each word in a sentence.

GLOSSARY

apartheid
a system of separation in South Africa under which nonwhite people went to separate schools and were not treated equally

colonial
relating to the period of time during which much of Africa was controlled and colonized by European countries and settlers

drought
a period of time with unusually low rainfall

equator
the imaginary line around the earth's surface that divides the Northern and Southern Hemispheres

indigenous
originating or occurring naturally in a particular place

insecticide
a substance used to kill insects

millet
a cereal plant that can be used to make flour

nomad
a person who moves from place to place

tectonic
relating to the structure of the earth's crust and the forces that cause the crust to move

LEARN MORE

Books

Aspen-Baxter, Linda. *Africa*. New York: Weigl
   Publishers, 2012.

Friedman, Mel. *Africa*. New York: Scholastic
   Publishing, 2009.

Winter, Jeanette. *Wangari's Trees of Peace: A True
   Story from Africa*. New York: Harcourt Brace,
   2008.

Web Links

To learn more about Africa, visit ABDO Publishing
Company online at **www.abdopublishing.com**.
Web sites about Africa are featured on our Book
Links page. These links are routinely monitored and
updated to provide the most current information
available.

Visit **www.mycorelibrary.com** for free additional tools
for teachers and students.

INDEX

Africa
  animals, 21–22
  farming, 33, 37–38
  history, 25–29
  natural resources,
    39–40
  people and culture,
    31–35
  plants, 19–20
  population, 17
  seismic activity, 15–16
  tourism, 38–39
AIDS, 40–41
Ancient Egypt, 25–26
Angola, 39
apartheid, 28
Atlas Mountains, 15

Botswana, 39

Congo River basin,
  19–20

Democratic Republic of
  Congo, 39

Ethiopian Highlands, 15
European colonization,
  27–28

Great Lakes, 16
Great Rift Valley, 15–16,
  22

Kalahari desert, 34
Kenya, 15, 33, 35

Maasai people, 33
Madagascar, 22
malaria, 40–41
Mandela, Nelson, 29
Mount Kilimanjaro, 8, 15
Namibia, 39
Niger River, 14
Nile River, 8, 17

rainforests, 13, 19–21

Sahara Desert, 8, 9, 14,
  34
Sahel, 14
San people, 34
savannas, 14, 16, 20
Senegal, 40
Serengeti Plain, 21–22
Siwa Oasis, 14
South Africa, 9, 28, 29,
  32

Tanganyika, Lake, 16
Tanzania, 15, 22, 33
Tuareg people, 34

Victoria, Lake, 16

Zimbabwe, 39, 40

ABOUT THE AUTHOR

Alicia Klepeis is a writer who began her career at the National Geographic Society. Her passion for travel has led her from Singapore to Sydney to Sumbawa. She now writes about international food, cool inventions, and world cultures.